Pathways to Lectio Divina

Methods from The Weave of Manquehue Prayer

MMXXI

To Mary,
Mother of Lectio Divina

'His mother stored up all these words in her heart'
(Luke 2: 19.51).

I would like ... to recall and recommend the ancient tradition of Lectio Divina ... If it is effectively promoted, this practice will bring to the Church – I am convinced of it – a new spiritual springtime.

BENEDICT XVI

First Published by The Weave of Manquehue Prayer 2021
www.weaveofmanquehue.org
theweave@manquehue.org

The right of Dom Leo Maidlow Davis and Cristóbal Valdés to be identified as authors of the works attributed to them has been asserted in accordance with the Copyright, Designs and Patents Act 1988

© The Weave of Manquehue Prayer 2021

The Weave of Manquehue Prayer
is a network of friends who seek to help one another
to pray, to cultivate friendship and to share with many the Good News of the Risen Christ. The Weave draws from the charism of the Manquehue Apostolic Movement to enrich initiatives of evangelisation and service.

Cover Picture:
Sandro Botticelli. Madonna of the Book (Madonna del Libro) *c.* 1483
Tempera on panel, 58 x 39.5 cm. Museo Poldi Pezzoli, Milan

Typeset by Antonia Shack
with contributions from
María Trinidad Pacheco Cepeda
and María Bernardita Opazo Illanes

Acknowledgements

Dom Leo Maidlow Davis, a monk of Downside Abbey, and Cristóbal Valdés, an Oblate of the Manquehue Apostolic Movement, have assembled the materials for this booklet. They are indebted for resources and advice to the monastic tradition of Lectio Divina, to the Manquehue Apostolic Movement and to friends linked by The Weave of Manquehue Prayer.

Nihil obstat   Rt Rev'd Dom Richard Yeo, MA, JCD
Imprimatur   ✠ Bishop Declan Lang, Bishop of Clifton, 25th June 2021

The *Nihil obstat* and *Imprimatur* are a declaration that a book or pamphlet is considered to be free from doctrinal or moral error. It is not implied that those who have granted the *Nihil obstat* and *Imprimatur* agree with the contents, opinions or statements expressed.

Contents

I. Introduction

    a. What is Lectio Divina?   1
    b. What is this Book About?   5

II. How to do Lectio Divina

    a. Preparing for Lectio Divina   8
    b. The Four Rungs of Lectio Divina   11
    c. The Echo   16

III. Shared Lectio Divina

    a. A Simple Method for Shared Lectio Divina   20
    b. Preparing Shared Lectio Divina   24
    c. A Method for a Celebration of the Word   29
    d. Online Lectio Divina   33

IV. Solitary Lectio Divina   35

    a. Scrutiny   38
    b. The Seven Readings   41
    c. Lectio Continua   44
    d. Random Readings   45

V. Honouring and Blessing your Bible   48

VI. Testimonies to the Power of the Word   50

VII. The Teaching of the Church on Lectio Divina   71

VIII. Seven Helpful Practices   85

IX. Recommended Reading   86

About the Cover Picture   90

I. Introduction

a. What is Lectio Divina?

JESUS CHRIST is risen and speaks to us today in Sacred Scripture. To engage in Lectio Divina or 'Divine Reading' is to read the Bible with the conviction that we can encounter Jesus our Saviour in those sacred pages. We will come to know him in Lectio Divina in the same way we see other men and women encountering him in the Gospels. During those days in the Holy Land, Jesus, the Light of the World, forgave sins and healed the sick, while teaching his disciples and leading them to eternal life. We will sit at Jesus' feet as Mary of Bethany did when he was visiting her home (Luke 10: 38-42). We must be ready to climb a tree, like Zacchaeus, and welcome him into our house and family (Luke 19: 1-10). We will go up the mountain with Peter, James and John and see the Lord Jesus in glory together with Moses and Elijah (Luke 9: 28-36). We shall hear the risen Christ speaking our name in the way only he can (John 20: 16). In Lectio Divina, Jesus Christ explains the Scriptures to us, just as to his two disciples on the road to Emmaus, making our hearts burn within us and leading us to the Eucharistic table (Luke 24: 13-35).

Lectio Divina is a particular way of reading the Bible. It calls for a different approach from the rapid reading that has become normal for us. In Lectio we will read the text slowly, moving word by word from verse to verse. We will reflect on the context of our passage, discover answers to our questions given in Sacred Scripture itself, listen to the resonances evoked, and investigate the footnotes and marginal references we may find. Moments of silence will make room for listening and for responding to God in prayer and in our life. Lectio Divina is reading in the power of the Holy Spirit, who frees, heals and gives us life. The Holy Spirit lifts us above the literal meaning of the text to listen to the voice of God, which deifies men and women by uniting them with Christ. Lectio Divina brings about a conversion from our empty minds obsessed by flesh and blood (cf. Matthew 16: 17b) to the mind of Christ, so that we can receive the ears, eyes and heart of Christ (Philippians 2: 5).

Lectio Divina is ancient. It is, in fact, the way in which the Fathers of the Church read the Scriptures in the first centuries. The majority of the classic texts about Lectio Divina were written in Greek or Latin, which have been the most widely and longest used languages in the Church. This is why you will find numerous Latin terms in these pages. You will also find encouragement in short quotations from the Fathers' writings. These brief extracts will attract you to deeper exploration of their life and teaching. The recent teaching of the Church, examples of which you can find in Section VII, will offer renewed inspiration for your Lectio Divina.

Since Lectio Divina has been practised throughout the Church from the earliest times, it is an accessible heritage for all Christians. Groups or individuals formed in different denominations can therefore gather for Lectio and grow in that unity for which Jesus prayed so intensely (John 17: 21-23). Moreover, we can bring those who are not Christians to Jesus in Lectio. It is enough to give the simple invitation, 'Come and see' (John 1: 46).

Although Lectio Divina is distinct from the academic study of the Bible, it is not opposed to it. Commentaries that deepen your understanding of the texts you read and pray with can enrich your Lectio. Lovers, after all, want to know as much as possible about their beloved. However, it is important to maintain the distinction between Lectio and study so that your Lectio does not become a detached analysis of God's word instead of the prayerful and personal encounter with him that is Lectio Divina. Always remember that prayer is the key to understanding the Bible.

The two illustrations that come with this book are to remind you to seek instruction from Mary in listening to the word of God. She shows us how we too can become a mother of Jesus. How is that? Jesus himself answers, 'My mother and my brothers are those who hear the word of God and put it into practice' (Luke 8: 21). This is exactly what Mary did. She now teaches us how to listen to and honour the word with a mother's care and love so that, with her, we can allow Christ to grow in us and, through us, to live and act for today's world.

Linocut by Javiera Rojas Bontempi

*Blessed are they who have Bethlehem in their heart,
in whose heart Christ is born each day!*
                        ST JEROME (*c.* 347-420)

Introduction

The Spirit ensures the Scriptures' perennial youth.
ST IRENAEUS (130 - *c.* 202)

b. What is this Book About?

We have called this book *Pathways to Lectio Divina: Methods from The Weave of Manquehue Prayer*. Although there are many excellent books on Lectio, there are not so many that provide detailed suggestions or pathways that you can follow to help you grow together with others in the practice of Lectio. Lectio Divina is reading God's Word in the community of the Church. To listen to God's word when you gather regularly as a local community will deepen your love for one another in Christ. This, in turn, will strengthen your community to proclaim Jesus Christ's Good News by the love of God made visible to those around you through your prayers, words and actions (cf. John 13: 34-35). Here, then, we offer you methods based on the experience of numerous groups belonging to or associated with the Manquehue Apostolic Movement, a lay Benedictine community founded in Santiago de Chile in 1977.

You will find Signposts and advice to help you follow the pathways developed over the years for both shared or group Lectio and solitary Lectio. Experience has shown that the best way to learn Lectio is to begin and make progress with the help of others, just as the Ethiopian eunuch was helped by the guidance of Philip (Acts 8: 27-39). It is not always easy to get started and it normally requires time and perseverance. Nevertheless, take heart, because no word comes from the mouth of the Lord without achieving in us the work he intended (Isaiah 55: 11).

It is most helpful to belong to a group that meets regularly, ideally every week. Time and perseverance, shared sufferings and joys, are needed for us to grow into friendship in Christ (cf. John 15: 12-17). We hope, therefore, that reading this book will encourage you to join or start a Lectio Divina group in your parish or at work, with family or friends, in a Travellers' community, in school, seminary or place of further study, in hospital or in prison, in person or online, just wherever you may be. Faithfulness to a group that gathers regularly for Lectio will soon lead you to want to read the Bible every day, because 'human beings live not on bread alone but on every word that comes from the mouth of the Lord' (Deuteronomy 8: 3). To move between group and solitary Lectio is not hard. You will discover that both are important for you.

This book has been published by The Weave of Manquehue Prayer, a network of friends who seek to help one another to pray, cultivate spiritual friendship and share with many the Good News of the Risen Christ. The Weave draws from the charism of the Manquehue Apostolic Movement to enrich initiatives of evangelization and service.

The friends in The Weave pray that this book will help you, through your practice of Lectio Divina, to deepen your friendship with Jesus Christ. You are invited to contact The Weave to find support and resources for yourself and for your group through their website or by email.

www.weaveofmanquehue.org

theweave@manquehue.org

Finally, you will find that looking up the biblical references given in this book will repay the trouble you take superabundantly.

II. How to do Lectio Divina

a. Preparing for Lectio Divina

Allocating Time to Read the Bible

Pray for the grace to find time for Lectio Divina every day, even if it is only for a single verse of the Bible, because 'Human beings do not live by bread alone, but on every word that comes from the mouth of God' (Matthew 4: 4). God's word is as necessary for your eternal life as food is for your body. Determine in advance when you will do your Lectio and for how long.

Just as regular meals are important, so is regularity in the time you give to Lectio Divina. Ask God for the grace to be faithful both in your commitment to the meetings of any Lectio group to which you belong and in your solitary reading.

If you are part of a Lectio Divina group, you can prepare for the next session by looking at the readings in advance, volunteering to prepare motivations and supporting the other activities that build up the community.

Choosing What to Read

It is good to allow the Lord to choose the subject matter of your time with him. One way of doing this is to follow the readings provided by the Church in her liturgy. You can find the Mass readings listed online or in your diocesan liturgical diary. Alternatively, you may read more extensively by taking, for example, the Gospel appointed for the year (Year A – Matthew; Year B – Mark; Year C – Luke), the book of Isaiah during Advent, or the Acts of the Apostles between Easter and Pentecost. Something to avoid is selecting a theme that you think fits your mood at the time. The Lord may have something different and better to share with you. Remember Martha's complaint to Jesus and his gentle response (Luke 10: 40-42).

Preparing a Place

Although you can read your Bible prayerfully in almost any place, it is helpful to have a special place for your Lectio as well as a regular time when you can expect to be free from distractions.

Lighting a candle helps you to remember that Christ is the Light of the World and recalls the candle that burnt at your Baptism. A crucifix or cross will show you how greatly God loves you: 'He gave his only Son, so that everyone who believes in him may not perish but may have eternal life' (John 3: 16). An icon or image of Our Lady or one of the Saints reminds you that you never do Lectio Divina alone; the whole Communion of Saints together with the Angels will be accompanying you. Taken together, these symbols remind us that it is into God's presence that we come when we approach his word. If we are using the readings for the coming Sunday or a special Feast, then we are also preparing for the Liturgy of the Word at Mass, which itself prepares us for the supreme encounter with Christ, the Word made Flesh, in the Liturgy of the Eucharist. Spreading a white cloth is a simple way of calling to mind the altar upon which the Eucharist is celebrated.

Silence

Treasure silence. In silence you will discover space to listen. The word you will hear comes to you personally and individually. As you prepare for Lectio, look forward to your meeting with Christ and allow his love for you to clear away your preoccupations and distractions (cf. Song of Songs 1: 4). Make yourself ready for the encounter with reverence and awe. God instructed Moses to take off his sandals as he approached him in the burning bush (Exodus 3: 1-6).

> *Unless, therefore, you come daily to the wells, unless you daily draw water, not only will you not be able to give a drink to others, but you yourself will also suffer a thirst for the word of God.*
>
> ORIGEN (*c.*184 - *c.*253)

> *Never approach the words of the mysteries that are in the Scriptures without praying and asking for God's help. Say, 'Lord, grant me to feel the power that is in them.' Reckon prayer to be the key that opens the true meaning of the Scriptures.*
>
> ISAAC OF NINEVEH (*c.* 613 - *c.* 700)

b. The Four Rungs of Lectio Divina

The best-known method for Lectio Divina is described in the late twelfth-century treatise of Guigo II (1114-1193), who was the ninth prior of the Grand Chartreuse. His *Ladder of Monks* gives his readers a ladder of four rungs that will help raise them through Lectio to contemplation. In this image, Lectio Divina moves from *lectio* (reading) to *meditatio* (meditation), from *meditatio* to *oratio* (praise and prayer), and concludes with *contemplatio* (wordless prayer). We will make use of Guigo's method to provide a structure for what follows because it helpfully outlines the process. However, it is important to understand that the ladder is not a rigid description of sequential stages. Ask in your prayer to remain always open and responsive to the impulses of the Holy Spirit, who knows what gifts are best for you and who blows where he pleases (John 3: 8).

You may be practising Lectio Divina in a group on or your own, but the fundamental pattern will remain similar.

i. *Lectio* – What the Passage Says

Read the chosen passage. The first rung or step of the ladder is to understand what the reading is about. The literal meaning of the text must always be our starting point. If it is a scene of activity, for example, you can begin by coming to understand the characters in the situation. Who are they? What are they doing? Where are they? When is the action happening? Why are the people involved saying what they are saying and doing what they are doing? Other kinds of scripture will invite different kinds of question.

Signposts

– Copy the text down.
– Explore the context of the passage.
– Write down all the ideas you can take from the text.
– Go through the passage verse by verse and then write down what you understand from each verse in your own words.
– Give your passage a title.

ii. *Meditatio* –What the Passage Says to Me

This step involves discovering what God is saying to you through the passage, here and now. This is because he has a word for you today. As you have come to understand what Jesus is saying to the people involved in the passage, so you will also hear what he is saying to you here and now in your own life. If you are distracted, recognise that the ideal conditions for doing Lectio Divina are, in truth, the ones you have now; your mood, your problems with your family, your work or studies, as well as your joys, tiredness or the boredom you are experiencing. Your awareness of the presence of God may be strong, or fragile and transient. Your situation is not so different from the people you are reading about on the sacred page. You are present with them.

At first, some passages may seem so familiar that you will be inclined to skim over them, but when you slow down you will always discover new treasures. If, after reading the passage, you immediately think of how it applies to someone else, go back to the passage and read it again, this time applying it to yourself. It is with your heart that God desires to speak (cf. Hosea 2: 16). Try to have the attitude of the boy Samuel who, when God called to him, had been taught to reply, 'Speak, Lord, for your servant is listening' (1 Samuel 3: 10).

> *The Word of God assures us divine remedies for the wounds of the soul, a protective shield against the darts of the enemy, the tools needed by a Christian, a priceless treasure that must not be buried.*
> ST BASIL OF CAESAREA (330-379)

Signposts

– Choose a verse that drew your attention or struck you in some way, perhaps by simple intuition. Copy it down. Try to discover why you have chosen these words. Is it because of the person described, a particular word or phrase, a situation, a gesture? Write down the reasons you can discern.

– Enter into your *Meditatio* with the help of some of these questions: 'What do I discover of God through this passage? What is the Good News that this word proclaims to me? What is the salvation (the healing, consolation, peace, grace and light) that this word brings to my life today? How does this passage illuminate my life? Does it change something in my way of seeing

things: my mood, my attitude or my disposition in certain situations?' Then ask, 'Lord, what are you saying to me in this reading today?' Write down the answers that come to you. Helped by these or other questions, think and pray.
– Commit a verse, phrase or even just a word to memory to treasure and dwell upon. This practice is known as *ruminatio* (chewing over repeatedly).

iii. *Oratio* –What am I to Say to God?

God is speaking to you personally. He is waiting for your answer. He wants to have a personal relationship with you, a conversation with you as you are and as you can be. You do not need to put up any barriers of pretence. Answer him faithfully. You can write down your own prayer. Your response may be simply staying with the word in silence. It may also be thanksgiving or praise, a petition, a blessing, a prayer of contrition, an intercession, or it may be a prayer of inspiration. It may be one single word, on which you pause and then repeat at will. Allow the Holy Spirit to pray in your heart.

Signposts

- – When you read, God speaks to you.
- – When you pray, you speak to God.
- – God listens, tell him everything.
- – God knows, do not say anything.

iv. *Contemplatio* – To be Wordless in the Presence of the Word

In Lectio Divina, you will sometimes be moved beyond words to a quiet and attentive resting in the presence of God. This can happen at any point in the process and, whenever it happens, accept it gladly.

When, as sometimes also happens, your contemplation slides back into preoccupation with your thoughts, then let go of them and simply return to *lectio,* the first rung of the ladder.

> *When a saying of the Lord's kindles the imagination of a hearer of the Word and makes him enamoured of the Wisdom that bursts into flames at the sight of any beauty, then 'the fire of the Lord is come down upon him'.*
>
> ORIGEN (*c.*184-*c.*253)

> *As the Word grows, words fall away.*
> ST AUGUSTINE (354-430)

Signposts

– Let God be God.
– Jesus Christ is the Bridegroom, the only Spouse of your soul; let him be so.
– If you are distracted, do not try to force *contemplatio*; just return to the first rung, *lectio*.

c. The Echo

In the Gospels, when people have had an encounter with Jesus, they cannot keep it to themselves. At the very beginning of his ministry, Jesus invites Andrew and his companion to come and see where he lives. After that meeting, 'The first thing Andrew did was to find his brother and say to him, "We have found the Messiah" ' (John 1: 41). After her conversation with Jesus at the well, the Samaritan woman hurries back to the town to tell the people, 'Come and see a man who has told me everything I have done ...' (John 4: 29). Jesus stays for two days with the Samaritans, who then say to the woman, 'Now we believe no longer because of what you told us; we have heard him ourselves and we know that he is indeed the Saviour of the world' (John 4: 42). On Easter morning, Mary of Magdala told the disciples, 'I have seen the Lord' (John 20: 18).

In shared Lectio Divina there is the special opportunity of briefly telling the echo you have in your heart to the other members of the group, just as Andrew, the Samaritans and Mary of Magdala did. Your echo is the resonance of your unique encounter with Christ; your opportunity to share the good news that he has brought to you as a gift you can impart to others.

If the idea of an echo is unfamiliar, it can help to think of it with some such image as this: when sound waves strike an object, they reverberate in uniquely different ways according to their own nature and to the nature, shape and location of the object they have struck. Children love to experiment with the echo of their shouts in a rocky valley or hanging wood. In a similar way, God's word will evoke a different response from each person in your group because everyone's heart and life are different. You will also find that your own response is different each time you encounter the same word of God. This is both because God's word is infinite and inexhaustible, and because your situation in life will have changed since your last encounter with that word.

Give your echo in the first person singular: 'This word says to *me* ... This word strikes *me* because ... It makes *me* think ... As *I* listened, *I* felt ... *I* believe ...'

Your echo is not an explanation, a speech or a homily based on the reading. It is not about applying the reading to somebody else or conjecturing how it might apply to someone in circumstances different from yours. Nor is it helpful to make a declaration of your spiritual or moral failings; rather an echo is your opportunity to proclaim what you hear Jesus, the Word of God, saying to you in the passage that you have just read. In this way you are sharing the good news of the Gospel.

> *For God's word offers different facets according to the capacity of the listener, and the Lord has portrayed his message in many colours, so that whoever gazes upon it can see in it what suits him.*
>
> ST EPHREM (306-373)

Echoes are not a conversation or a discussion about Christ as though he were absent. Experience has shown that to keep the focus on Christ's presence it is better not to ask a question or to answer the questions of others. Discussion of obscurities or the imparting of specialist knowledge about the passage can take place outside the Lectio session. Lectio Divina is prayer and needs to be distinguished from Bible study. In shared Lectio, the group leader has the important role of gently leading the members back, whenever they have begun to stray, to a prayerful awareness of Christ's presence in their midst.

> *The stream of holy Scripture flows not from human investigation but from revelation by God.*
> ST BONAVENTURE (1221-1274)

It is not compulsory to share an echo, and echoes should not be a way of avoiding what may seem an awkward silence. Sometimes silence is the most profound response you can give. Nonetheless, when a word has truly struck you it is important to bear witness to that and invite others to share your joy.

Sharing echoes has the power to transform your group into a community. The echoes of the other people help you to deepen your love of God through your deepening love of them. Because the Holy Spirit inspires our echoes, to share your echo is an expression of the love of God.

This is the nature of love: to the extent that we distance ourselves from the centre of the circle and do not love God, we distance ourselves from our neighbours: but if we love God, then the nearer we draw to him in love, the more we are united with our neighbour in love.

DOROTHEUS OF GAZA (*c.* 505- *c.* 565)

Signposts

– You have listened to Jesus. Tell others what he has said to you.

– Give your echo in the first person singular (I, me).

– Enjoy silence; the Holy Spirit inspires silence as well as echoes.

– Leave questions and discussions for another time.

– Listen to the echoes of others with the ear of your heart; their echoes are also a word from God for you.

III. Shared Lectio Divina

a. A Simple Method for Shared Lectio Divina

Here is an accessible way to do Lectio Divina in a small group, perhaps of friends or family, at school or in a parish. It requires only simple preparation and the participants can come with little or no experience of Lectio. First, you will find a brief introductory description and some recommendations; then we will provide a simple Order of Service that you can easily follow. To be clear about what to do, read this whole section through to the end of the Order of Service.

A session of shared Lectio needs a leader. This can be either a permanent appointment or someone chosen specially for each session. Sharing Lectio can be quite informal; you can do it, for instance, while out in the country, visiting friends or travelling. This method also works well for a group that meets regularly, ideally every week.

If possible, prepare the place for Lectio Divina with symbols, such as a cross, a white tablecloth and a candle.

The motivation that precedes the reading of the chosen Scripture passage is a brief invitation to put aside any distractions or anxieties that might prevent people from listening to God's word with their full attention. It should not be a sermon, but it should draw the participants' attention to anything that can help deepen their engagement with the words they are going to hear. In section b (p. 24) you will find further directions to help you compose a motivation, but for this simple form of shared Lectio a few words of encouragement to listen will suffice. For daily Lectio, or if you have not been able to prepare a motivation, it is good to employ St Benedict's exhortation, which you will find on p. 28.

The period of silent prayer that follows the motivation should be long enough for the participants to become calm and focused; one minute is a minimum.

Either the leader or someone appointed by the leader reads the whole Scripture passage. After a pause for silent reflection, the leader or another person reads the passage again, verse by verse or section by section, depending on where breaks most naturally occur. Allow a pause for silence in between verses or sections to make room for prayer and personal responses or echoes. Alternatively, you may prefer to read the passage only once, leaving a substantial period of silence of several minutes before echoes are invited. Some groups like to read the passage two or three times, each time with a different reader, whose unique way of reading may reveal different facets for the listeners. A gentle knock from the leader can indicate that the time for echoes has arrived. After the echoes, you have an opportunity to offer Bidding Prayers similar to those made at Mass or at Lauds and Vespers.

Before the concluding Sign of Peace, ask the prayers of Our Lady and of other saints, such as the Saint you may have chosen as a patron for your Lectio Divina group or the Saint of the day.

Here to help you now is a brief Order of Service:

Order of Service for Shared Lectio Divina

The service begins with the Sign of the Cross

> All: In the name of the Father, and of the Son, and of the Holy Spirit. Amen.

Invocation of the Holy Spirit

> ℣. Come, Holy Spirit, fill the hearts of your faithful, and kindle in them the fire of your love. Send forth your Spirit and they shall be created,
> ℟. and you shall renew the face of the earth.

Penitential Rite

> ℣. To prepare ourselves to listen to the word of the Lord, let us call to mind our sins:
> *Pause for reflection.*
> ℣. You were sent to heal the contrite of heart: Lord, have mercy
> ℟. Lord, have mercy.
> ℣. You came to call sinners: Christ, have mercy
> ℟. Christ, have mercy.
> ℣. You are seated at the right hand of the Father to intercede for us: Lord, have mercy
> ℟. Lord, have mercy.

Shared Lectio Divina

All: May almighty God have mercy on us, forgive us our sins, and bring us to everlasting life. Amen.

(You can also use any of the other penitential rites you will find in the Missal.)

Then the motivation is given by one of those who have prepared it.

A period of silent prayer follows the motivation.

Lectio Divina

The chosen passage of Scripture is read aloud according to the method you have chosen.
Silent reflection and echoes now follow.
Bidding Prayers may now be offered.

Our Father

The Our Father is briefly introduced with a formula similar to that used at Mass.
All recite the Our Father slowly together.

Conclusion

℣. May the Lord bless us, keep us from all evil and bring us to eternal life.

℟. Amen.

℣. Mary, Mother of Lectio Divina,

℟. Pray for us.

℣. St N. (Patron of the group, saint of the day or other)

℟. Pray for us.

Conclude by exchanging a sign of peace.

b. Preparing Shared Lectio Divina

Motivations and Invitations

Motivations and *Invitations* are always helpful when a group gathers for Lectio Divina.

Motivations are words that remind the group that Christ is Risen and that he speaks through his word, drawing everyone into an attitude of attentive listening. Motivations are a personal invitation to listen, coming from someone who cannot wait for others to hear what she has heard so that their joy will make hers complete. A motivation usually includes gentle reminders, questions, keys for understanding and pointers to relate to the readings. They are carefully prepared beforehand but are normally best spoken from the heart rather than read out word for word. The motivation to a reading should not be longer than this paragraph (*c*. 150 words). In a Celebration of the Word, a General Motivation should be no more than four times longer (*c*. 600 words).

Good motivations direct people's attention towards the readings, not to the motivations themselves. They are like John the Baptist, who prepares the way of the Lord and points to Jesus, saying, 'He must grow greater, I must grow less' (John 3: 30). Motivations are not sermons or lectures. They are not personal testimonies or echoes. They do not try to explain the readings or put them into other words. Instead, they are like a menu that whets our appetite and makes us look forward to the meal.

Motivations play a key role in the Celebration of the Word that we will describe in the following section, but they can also be freely included in less elaborate moments of shared Lectio Divina. In this way you can enrich the simple method proposed in the previous section with one or more prepared motivations.

Invitations can also enrich shared Lectio Divina. An invitation is no more than one sentence, or at most two, that introduces elements such as the echoes, the Creed or the Our Father. Invitations link these elements with the theme of the meeting. They can be spontaneous but are best composed beforehand.

Who Prepares?

Preparing a moment of shared Lectio Divina is normally the task of two members of the group, who take on the responsibility in turns so that all the members eventually have the opportunity of performing this service.

Preparation is usually a prayerful experience in its own right as well as a precious moment for the cultivation of spiritual friendship among the members of a group. If necessary, you can prepare individually, but doing it in pairs will bear abundant fruit. Preparing at least one or two days ahead of the actual meeting allows the work to mature in your heart.

A Preparation Guide

The preparation guide that follows assumes you are preparing a Celebration of the Word for the coming Sunday's readings, but it can be adapted if you are using other texts or preparing a less elaborate meeting.

1. Get ready. Find the readings for next Sunday. Close your door, turn off your phone, have your Bible, pen and paper at hand. Put your working space in order. Bring a cross, light a candle. Read together the section on motivations and invitations given above.
2. Begin with the sign of the cross, a moment of silent prayer (1 or 2 minutes) and the invocation of the Holy Spirit.
3. Take turns to read aloud each of the three readings, allowing a period of silence for personal notes in between. You may also want to include the Responsorial Psalm.
4. Share what you have written and then search together for one overarching theme for the Celebration of the Word.
5. Choose three key elements to be included in the General Motivation, and one key element for the motivation for each reading.
6. Choose one opening and one final hymn.
7. Allocate tasks. The list of tasks to be allocated for a Celebration of the Word will look like this:
    – General Motivation
    – Prayers for forgiveness
    – Motivation for the First Reading
    – Motivation for the Second Reading

- Motivation for the Gospel
- Invitation to share echoes
- Invitation to say the Creed
- Bidding prayers with an invitation
- Invitation to say the Our Father
- Printing a handout with the references to the readings and the lyrics of the hymns
- Preparing the place: white cloth, cross, candle, flowers, and, if possible, a lectern. Beauty and order are important. If the Celebration is online, prepare some slides.

8. Finish your preparation by saying the Our Father.

Preparation like this normally takes around 45 minutes working together and another 30 minutes working individually.

The Exhortation of St Benedict

St Benedict wrote his Rule for Monks in the early sixth century. In the Prologue to his Rule, he exhorts his readers to wake up to the reality of God. It is a powerful summons to every Christian, and not just to monks. You will find his words are a model motivation; indeed, you may decide to use them when there has been no opportunity of preparing a specific motivation for a shared Lectio session.

And so let us at long last arise,
because Scripture is waking us and calls out,
'Now is the moment for us to rise from sleep.'
With our eyes open to God's own light
and our ears ringing,
let us hear what his voice is teaching us as,
each day,
he calls out and says,
'Today, if you wish to hear his voice,
do not make your hearts hard.'
And, once more,
'Whoever has ears to hear,
let him hear what the Spirit is saying to the churches.'
And what does the Spirit say?
'Come, children, listen to me.
I shall teach you to fear the Lord.
Run while you have your life's light,
before the night of death overtake you.'

RULE OF ST BENEDICT, PROLOGUE, vv. 8-13

c. A Method for a Celebration of the Word

A Celebration of the Word follows a method similar to the one presented in the previous section, but is more elaborate and requires more preparation. It is particularly appropriate as the preparation of a group or family for Sunday or special Feast Day Masses. A Celebration of the Word can also mark important occasions in our lives, such as the reception of Sacraments, anniversaries, births and deaths or anything else significant. If shared Lectio Divina is a spiritual meal, then the Celebration of the Word is a spiritual feast. Care taken over the preparation of the room will intensify the experience. A table with a white cloth, candles and a cross or crucifix will call to mind the Eucharist as the summit to which the Celebration of the Word is pointing. A lectern will give prominence to the proclamation of God's Word. Flowers and appropriately coloured carpets or hangings, holy water, icons or statues deepen the participants' awareness of being caught up in the Communion of Saints. An atmosphere of silence, order, beauty and prayerfulness should reign.

Although the Celebration of the Word follows the method given in the previous section on shared Lectio Divina, you will find the following Order of Service helpful. Many groups and communities have used it regularly.

An Order of Service for a Celebration of the Word

The service begins with the Sign of the Cross:

> All: In the name of the Father, and of the Son, and of the Holy Spirit. Amen.

General Motivation

All stand.

Invocation of the Holy Spirit

> ℣. Come, Holy Spirit, fill the hearts of your faithful, and kindle in them the fire of your love. Send forth your Spirit and they shall be created,
> ℟. and you shall renew the face of the earth.

Opening Hymn

Penitential Rite[1]

Three prayers for forgiveness are said, each followed by a section of the Kyrie:

℣. Lord, have mercy	℟. Lord, have mercy.
℣. Christ, have mercy	℟. Christ, have mercy.
℣. Lord, have mercy	℟. Lord, have mercy.

> ℣. May almighty God,
> ℟. have mercy on us, forgive us our sins, and bring us to everlasting life.

First and Second Reading

---

[1] The Penitential Rite can be adapted to the theme of the Celebration. This encourages deeper listening and consideration of the barriers that are preventing us from welcoming Christ and his word as well as leading us to repentance for our sins.

Sit for the first two readings.
Motivation to the reading

℣. A reading from the book of N./ from the letter to N.

The reading

℣. The word of the Lord.

℟. Thanks be to God.

After each reading, pause to reflect on what it is saying to you. Do not share echoes at this stage.

Gospel

Motivation. After the motivation all stand.

℣. A reading from the holy Gospel according to N.

℟. Glory to you, O Lord.

The Gospel

℣. The Gospel of the Lord.

℟. Praise to you, Lord Jesus Christ.

℣. Through the words of the Gospel may our sins be wiped away.

℟. Amen.

Silence and Echoes

All sit for a period of personal reflection and prayer. An invitation to share ends the silence and opens the time for echoes.

Creed[2]

---

[2] You can use either the Niceno-Constantinopolitan Creed or the Apostles' Creed. You will find both in your missal. The Apostles' Creed is the ancient Baptismal Creed that is an easily remembered summary of our faith.

After the echoes, all stand in response to an invitation to recite the Creed.

Bidding Prayers[3]

There follows an invitation to offer Bidding Prayers. After each prayer:

℣. Lord, in your mercy,

℟. Hear our prayer.

Our Father

After the Bidding Prayers, all are invited to recite the Our Father.

Final Hymn

Final Blessing

℣. May the Lord bless us, keep us from all evil and bring us to everlasting life.

℟. Amen.

Sign of Peace

Hail Mary

Invocation of the Patron Saint of the group

℣. St N. (Patron of the group, saint of the day or other)

℟. Pray for us.

---

[3] A brief invitation leads into the Bidding Prayers, starting with those that have been prepared. Four prayers are usually sufficient: for the Universal Church, the Local Church, those in need, and the community present at the Celebration. Other members of the group may then wish to offer spontaneous prayers.

Occasionally it will be helpful to prolong the Celebration with an Agape, a joyful sharing of food and drink that will deepen the members' friendship in Christ. Great care must be taken to ensure that no one feels excluded (cf. 1 Corinthians 11: 17-22).

Many groups discover that a call to some service or mission arises naturally from the community life that their Lectio Divina is creating.

d. Online Lectio Divina

The COVID-19 pandemic has obliged many existing Lectio Divina groups to move their sessions online. They have discovered that in this new situation many people, who could not previously attend because of their remoteness or confinement to their home, are able to take part. Online Lectio Divina groups can involve participants from all around the world. This has been an unexpected blessing.

The online format has proved helpful for weekly Lectio groups, Celebrations of the Word on special Feasts and occasions, as well as daily online scrutiny, which will be described under solitary Lectio Divina. On The Weave of Manquehue Prayer website you can find information about online Open Lectio and other opportunities available in this format.

Nonetheless, it remains true that physical meetings are best for gathering in Christ. We can look forward in hope to the joy of meeting in person the people we have come to know online. With them, we will be able to share important aspects of our lives, such as celebratory meals or times of sadness and consolation, and with them we may develop a mission of service to the world beyond our group.

> *We are fruitful when what we hear and sing we also do. For hearing is our sowing, and our doing is the fruit of our sowing.*
>
> ST AUGUSTINE (354-430)

IV. Solitary Lectio Divina

So far, we have given much of our attention to Lectio Divina in a group. This practice has great advantages and strengths and is normally the best way to learn Lectio Divina. However, it can be hard to find or set up a Lectio Divina group and many people do not have ready access to the Internet. Furthermore, once you realise that Lectio Divina is to be a crucial part of your life, you will want to practise it frequently, which will often mean reading God's word on your own. You will find that this way of reading has special qualities that you will come to value. To begin with, solitary Lectio is easy to embark on; all you need is your Bible, yourself and some time. You can turn to Lectio at odd moments in the day, whether at work or at home. To have prayed with your Bible in a holy place or somewhere that is beautiful or otherwise significant will become a precious memory. Equally, you will want to turn to your Bible in moments of distress and sorrow, when making decisions or on important occasions. The Bible is the best company for trips and times of waiting. Just as solitary prayer and prayer in community are complementary, so are solitary and shared Lectio Divina.

> *We speak to him when we pray; we listen to him when we read his word.*
>
> ST AMBROSE (*c.* 340-397)

Here follow four methods that work well when you are engaged in solitary Lectio Divina.

a. **Scrutiny** is focused and concentrated, allowing for deep penetration, both your penetration into the word and the word's penetration into your heart. In the Manquehue Apostolic Movement it is the usual method for daily Lectio, with echoes being shared at the end. It calls for a substantial period of time, at least thirty minutes, a proper place, your Bible, a Lectio notebook and something with which to write. It is laborious, but your trouble will find ample reward.

b. **The Seven Readings** is a more extensive exercise and will enable you to explore the Bible in its entirety.

As with all methods of Lectio, it will benefit from an allocated slot of time. However, a special gift of the Seven Readings is that you will always have something to read from your Bible, whether you have at your disposal only a few minutes or a whole morning. Besides, you need only a Bible, which makes it is an easily portable method: you can move ahead with your Seven Readings on a train journey, while waiting for someone or almost anywhere.

c. **Lectio Continua** will both extend and deepen your acquaintance with God's word as you devote time and attention to a single book of the Bible, getting to know it and its author in a fuller way than is possible by reading only selected passages.

d. **Random Readings** feature in the lives of many Saints and ordinary Christians. They are a way of inviting the Lord to illuminate a particular situation. It is wise to approach this practice with caution in case it degenerates from openness to God's word into a superstitious hunting for quick answers to situations that may be calling for careful discernment, perhaps with others, and your deep response.

Though methods are useful and often necessary, Lectio Divina is not a method; it is a relationship. Therefore, you can be flexible as you move from one method to another in different circumstances. It can help to combine methods, even intertwining the ones proposed for shared Lectio with those indicated for solitary Lectio.

Changing or adapting a method may sometimes help to avoid a sense of repetitiveness or boredom. Feel free to change, but not too easily, because some methods require time and perseverance to bear fruit. You may strike the right balance, for example, by linking changes to liturgical seasons or other events in your life.

You will soon come to realise that there is a close affinity between solitary Lectio Divina and Silent Prayer, which is also known as Contemplative Prayer. A period of silence before Lectio, and sometimes a long one, may become indispensable for you. You may feel the need to hold your Bible or have it in sight during silent prayer. Your silence will lead you to reading and your reading to silence. Sometimes you may be moved to repeat slowly a single word or phrase. One form of prayer nourishes the other, while both integrate with liturgical prayer, in this way enabling your union with the Lord to mature and deepen as you are drawn into the sacramental life of Christ's Mystical Body.

The practice of repeating a word or phrase from the Bible, for some minutes, days or even years, is an ancient one. The early monks called it *ruminatio* (chewing over repeatedly): it consists in committing a word to memory and bringing it back to mind throughout the day, to 'chew' it again and again by gentle and loving repetition, either silently or in a low voice. You will easily find opportunities to recall your word, such as when you are on the bus, doing house chores, exercising or even sleeping. Many find it helps to repeat their word or phrase in time to the passing of the beads of a rosary through their fingers.

a. Scrutiny

To scrutinise means 'to search, investigate, examine in detail'. It is a way of going through the different books of the Bible with the intention of meeting Jesus Christ in his word. It involves an attitude of active listening. St Benedict opens his Rule with the words 'Listen carefully, O son, to the instructions of your Master; incline the ear of your heart. Freely accept and fulfil in your actions the advice of the Father who loves you, so that you may return to him through the hard work of obedience, from whom you have strayed through the sloth of disobedience' (*Rule of St Benedict*, Prologue, v. 1).

We recommend the Study Edition of the New Jerusalem Bible because, alongside the text of the book, there are accompanying notes with a small letter [a]. These letters correspond to notes at the foot of the page. There are also marginal references that clarify the text in different ways. Both footnotes and marginal references are most useful as a guide towards other texts involving similar themes or to readings that have new references that develop the same idea.

A Method for Scrutiny

1. Find a comfortable place where you can sit, read and write. Set time aside for scrutinising and put away your phone and other distractions. Make sure you have your Study Edition of the New Jerusalem Bible, a pen and your notebook.
2. Start with a prayer to the Holy Spirit.
3. Make a humble admission of your sins to God and praise him for his mercy and forgiveness.
4. Keep a time of silence, at least one minute. If you are familiar with Silent Prayer, allow a time for it before reading.
5. Read the passage in its entirety.
6. Choose a verse or a part of the reading that particularly strikes you and copy it down with loving care. Copying is a simple but powerful way of reading attentively. See if there are any marginal references or footnotes for that part of the reading. Choose one of them and go to the indicated passage. Copy the verses that speak to you. You can move on from there to another text and so on, or you

can go back to a previous text or start again from another part of the original text. If you do not know where to start, copy and scrutinise from the beginning of your original text and use your time to progress slowly down the passage and its references. Do not try to read a lot; just make sure you read well.

7. Stop and pray when the Holy Spirit moves you. Allow yourself time for chewing over (meditating on) any passage that has a resonance in your heart. You may also want to pray with words or in writing. Do not be afraid to write directly to the Three Persons of the Trinity and to Our Lady and the Saints, as many Christians have throughout history.

8. Save two or three minutes before your time is up to review what you have written. You may want to underline something or write some final notes.

9. Conclude by slowly praying the Our Father.

10. Ask the prayers of Mary, Mother of God, the Saint of the day or the Saint you may have chosen as a patron for your Lectio Divina group.

Scrutinising alongside others, even if online, is a great help in keeping focused. In this case, you can use the order of service of the Simple Method for shared Lectio Divina (p. 22) up to step 5 above, share echoes between steps 8 and 9, and finish with a sign of peace.

If you scrutinise regularly, you will want to have a special notebook and review it prayerfully from time to time.

b. The Seven Readings

The Seven Readings is a way of reading the Bible in its entirety and of discovering Christ, the Word of God, whom you will slowly come to recognise all through the Bible, though he is often concealed in the Old Testament and more fully revealed only in the New. With the Seven Readings, you will be able to perceive the harmony that resonates through all parts of the Bible, one passage vibrating in harmony or counterpoint with another, this text foreshadowing that, and that opening for you unexpected layers of meaning in the first. The Word itself illuminates and explains the Word.

> *Then, having banished all worldly concerns and thoughts, strive in every way to devote yourself constantly to the sacred reading so that continuous meditation will seep into your soul and, as it were, will shape it to its image, and thus Scripture transforms you into its own likeness.*
> JOHN CASSIAN (360-435)

Begin by dividing your Bible up into the following seven parts, marking them with ribbons or coloured adhesive page markers, which you can find at a stationer's.

1. The Pentateuch (Genesis to Deuteronomy)
2. The Historical Books (Joshua to 2 Maccabees)
3. The Wisdom Books (Job to Sira [Ecclesiasticus])

4. The Lyrical Books (Psalms, the Song of Songs, and Lamentations)
5. The Prophets (Isaiah to Malachi)
6. The Gospels (Matthew to John)
7. The rest of the New Testament (Acts to Revelation)

Following the steps given below, start reading from the beginning of the Pentateuch, then jump to the Historical Books, then to the Wisdom Books and so on. When you have read from the seventh part, go back to the first part and pick it up from where you finished the last time you were there. Do not omit any verse, but just read patiently through lists of ancient names and repetitive and apparently meaningless descriptions. Do not think you have to find something useful or something to do, just be there, and read on. When you get to the end of one of the seven parts, move your mark back to the beginning of it. You will not finish all seven parts at the same time, but you will always have a mark in each of the seven. Eventually, you will have read the whole Bible.

The Seven Readings is a more extensive way of reading than Scrutinizing. You may read one, two or three headings in one of the seven parts at a time, according to the time you have and the characteristics of the text. Ideally, you will read from several of the seven parts at any one time, but sometimes you will be able to read from only one or two. Allow the Holy Spirit to guide you and remember that it is never about how much you read, but rather about reading with as much care and love as you can.

Give particular attention to the signs of God's love. Each time you come across something that speaks of God's love, of his life, truth, goodness or omnipotence, pause to say the Our Father, the prayer that Jesus himself taught us. Then continue reading.

Ignorance of the Scriptures is ignorance of Christ.
ST JEROME (*c.*347-420)

A Method for the Seven Readings

1. Begin with the sign of the cross.
2. Say a prayer to the Holy Spirit.
3. Be silent for at least one minute to become aware of God's presence. The Father is present and sees and knows all you need (cf. Matthew 6: 6.8b). Bring your silence to an end with the doxology that concludes the Eucharistic Prayers: *Through him, and with him, and in him, O God, almighty Father, in the unity of the Holy Spirit, all glory and honour is yours, for ever and ever. Amen.*
4. Start reading from the appropriate part and, after a while, move on to the next one, and so on. Remember to pray an Our Father each time you see a sign of God's love and then continue reading.
5. At the end of the time, keep a moment of silence and finish with an Our Father.
6. Then say: 'Mary, Mother of Lectio Divina, pray for us.' You may add any other saint whose prayers you wish to invoke.

> *You who are accustomed to assist at the divine mysteries know well that it is necessary to guard with the greatest care and respect the body of the Lord that you receive, lest the least particle be lost, lest anything that has been consecrated fall to the ground. Do you perchance think that it is a lesser fault to treat negligently the Word of God, which is God's Body?*
> ST GREGORY THE GREAT (*c.* 540-604)

You will find that the order of books is not the same in all Bibles, which can affect how you split up the seven parts.

You may also find that some non-Catholic editions of the Bible omit the books called deutero-canonical, that is, Judith, Tobit, 1 and 2 Maccabees, Wisdom, Sira [Ecclesiasticus], Baruch, and the parts of Daniel that exist only in Greek. Since these books are used in the Catholic liturgy and are alluded to by the New Testament and the Fathers, you probably want to find a Bible that includes them.

c. Lectio Continua

St Benedict advises his monks to take one book from the Bible during Lent and read it through completely, from beginning to end (*per ordinem ex integro*). It was not until the 13th century that a Bible could be contained in a single volume and, even then, the format was expensive and inconvenient: for centuries, therefore, people have been reading the Bible a book at a time. If we read only small sections of the Bible, we lose the opportunity of developing a profound relationship with the component books and their authors, who will enrich and enlarge us with what is unfamiliar in them. As we make the journey through the wilderness to the Promised Land, seeking God, he will show us wonders we never knew, 'for my thoughts are not your thoughts and your ways are not my ways' (Isaiah 55: 8). To explore an entire book calls for preparation and careful consideration of which book to choose. To help, here are some suggestions:

– The Gospel of Luke, a chapter a day, from 1st to 24th December.

– A letter of St Paul, such as Romans or Galatians, during Lent.

– The Acts of the Apostles during Eastertide.

– The Book of Tobit when you are on a journey.

As a Method for Lectio Continua you can use the arrangement proposed for the Seven Readings (p. 43), or an adaptation of the Simple Method for Shared Lectio Divina (p. 20).

d. Random Readings

We know from the lives and writings of the Saints that they have sometimes turned to the Bible for help by way of a reading discovered at random. You will find numerous incidents in *Testimonies to the Power of the Word* (pp. 50-70).

If you are moved by the Spirit to take a reading at random, it is important that the ear of your heart be open to what the Lord may say to you at that moment. Avoid resorting to random readings as short cuts in making challenging or vital decisions or out of mere curiosity. Instead, they should indicate a readiness to renounce our own initiative and submit ourselves wholly to God's word. We do not see the Saints treating the Bible in a superstitious or magical way, with the mentality of someone turning to a horoscope. Often they hear the reading that comes to them unchosen in the context of the Liturgy, and especially during the Eucharist. They are nearly always already engaged in a dialogue with the Word of God, and this engagement has prepared them to hear what is going to deepen their vocation. We find the attitude of these listeners described for us in Psalm 85 [84]: 8 – 'I am listening. What is God's message?'

You may feel the impulse to take a reading at random from your Bible at moments of special significance, such as reaching the goal of a pilgrimage, coming to the end of an important meeting, when a friend arrives or departs or when you are embarking on an important new stage in your life. Random readings can be taken when alone or with others.

Here is a suggested method for a Random Reading:

1. Invoke the Holy Spirit. You may also ask the Lord for a word through the intercession of Our Lady and say the *Hail Mary*.
2. Take a reading at random from the Bible.
3. Spend time in silent reflection.
4. Say the Our Father.

V. Honouring and Blessing your Bible

The more you dedicate yourself to Lectio Divina, the more your reverence for the book of the Bible itself will grow. Bachiarius, a fifth-century Spanish monk, wrote, 'The Bible is Jesus Christ wrapped in linen cloths of parchment.' As you carry your Bible with you more often, you may want to make or buy a case to protect it and to signify your reverence for God's living Word. Bible cases are commercially available, and instructions for making your own are easy to find online. Holding your Bible, handling it reverently and having it close to you will become more important. Even looking at your Bible as you are engaged in other activities can bring you into the Lord's presence.

If you would like to have your Bible blessed, here is a prayer of blessing that can be used:

℣. Our help is in the name of the Lord.
℟. Who made heaven and earth.
℣. The Lord be with you.
℟. And with your spirit.

Let us pray.
God our Father,
grant, we pray,
that N. (*name of the person whose Bible is being blessed*)

and all who read this Bible
will be guided by the Holy Spirit
to listen with a quiet heart to your living Word.
May the Risen Christ open their mind
to understand the Scriptures,
to grow in joy and wonder
as they learn of your Creation
and witness the faithful love
you have revealed to your people.
Lead them ever more deeply
into the mystery of the new birth and eternal life
that the Paschal Sacrifice of your beloved Son
has won for them.
Who lives and reigns with you
in the unity of the Holy Spirit,
God, for ever and ever.
℞. Amen.

May God, whose Word makes all things holy,
pour out his blessing upon this Bible
and any who use it, in the name of the Father,
and of the Son, ✠ and of the Holy Spirit. ℞. Amen.

VI. Testimonies to the Power of the Word

The following passages, arranged chronologically, show how crucial Lectio Divina has been in the lives of holy men and women. Reading them will encourage you in your own practice of Lectio Divina.

Origen (*c.*184 – *c.*253)

TO UNDERSTAND THE THINGS OF GOD, WHAT IS ABSOLUTELY NECESSARY IS PRAYER.

*Origen was born into a fervent Christian family in Alexandria; his father, who was martyred when Origen was seventeen, had introduced him while still very young to the Bible. Origen's influence as a Bible scholar has been immense in both the East and the West. He maintained that understanding Scripture demands, even more than study, closeness to Christ and prayer. He was convinced that there could be no authentic knowledge of Christ apart from growth in his love. Here Origen is writing a letter to the youthful Gregory (c. 213-270), who, when he became Bishop of Neocaesarea, would be known as Thaumaturgus, the 'wonder worker' (*Epistola ad Gregorium, 3: PG 11, 92*). He gives him this advice:*

Devote yourself to the Lectio of the divine Scriptures; apply yourself to this with perseverance. Do your reading with the intent of believing in and pleasing God. If during the

Lectio you encounter a closed door, knock and it will be opened to you by that guardian of whom Jesus said, 'The gatekeeper will open it for him' (cf. John 10: 3). By applying yourself in this way to Lectio Divina, search diligently and with unshakable trust in God for the meaning of the divine Scriptures, which is hidden in great fullness within. You ought not, however, to be satisfied merely with knocking and seeking: to understand the things of God, what is absolutely necessary is prayer. For this reason, the Saviour told us not only: 'Seek and you will find', and 'Knock and it shall be opened to you', but also added, 'Ask and you shall receive' (Matthew 7: 7-8).

St Antony of Egypt (251-356)

THE PASSAGE HAD BEEN READ ON HIS ACCOUNT.

The Life of Antony was written by St Athanasius (c. 296–373), Bishop of Alexandria for 45 years. Athanasius spent his life defending the divinity of Christ against the Arian heresy, a struggle for which he had to endure five periods of exile. His Life of Antony *was immensely popular and helped spread the monastic way of life to the wider Church. It would have a big impact on St Augustine. This passage is from the opening chapter of* The Life of Antony.

Antony, you must know, was by descent an Egyptian: his parents were of good family and possessed considerable wealth, and, as they were Christians, he also was reared in the same faith. After the death of his father and mother, he was left alone with one little sister: his age was about eighteen or twenty, and on him the care both of home and sister rested. Now it was not six months after the death of his parents, and going according to custom into the Lord's House, he communed with himself and reflected as he walked how the Apostles left all and followed the Saviour; and how they in the Acts sold their possessions and brought and laid them at the Apostles' feet for distribution to the needy, and what and how great a hope was laid up for them in heaven. Pondering over these things, he entered the church, and it happened the Gospel was being read, and he heard the Lord saying to the rich man, 'If you would be perfect, go and sell all that you have and give to the poor; and come follow me and you shall have treasure in heaven.' Antony, as though God had put him in mind of the Saints, and the passage had been read on his account, went out immediately from the church, and gave the possessions of his forefathers to the villagers — they were three hundred acres, productive and very fair — that they should be no more a clog upon himself and his sister. And all the rest that was movable he sold, and having got together much money he gave it to the poor, reserving a little, however, for his sister's sake.

And again, as he went into the church, hearing the Lord say in the Gospel, 'be not anxious for the morrow', he could stay no longer, but went out and gave those things also to the poor.

St Ambrose (*c.*340-397)

YOU FILL BOTH MORNING AND EVENING WITH JOY.

In 374 Ambrose, the young Governor of Northern Italy, was made Bishop of Milan by popular acclaim and to his great surprise; he was just a catechumen, still preparing for baptism. Although he tried to escape this responsibility, he turned out to be an outstanding bishop. Like Athanasius, he was tireless in his opposition to Arianism. His converts included St Augustine. He encouraged his congregation to join in the singing of the psalms and he incorporated the use of hymns into Christian worship. In this commentary on Psalm 118 (119 in the Hebrew Bible) (Sermo 19, 30-32: CSEL 63, 437-439) *St Ambrose urges us to rise early to meditate on God's word so as to greet the Risen Christ, the Sun of Justice.*

How abundant is the grace of the Church, how great the rewards of a living faith! Since these invite us, let us forestall the rising sun to greet Christ, the Sun of Justice, before he can say: 'See, here I am.' He both wants and expects us to be there before him.

You can hear Christ's desire and expectation expressed in his words to the angel of the church of Pergamum: 'Repent, or I will soon come to you', and to the angel of Laodicea: 'Be zealous and repent. See, I stand at the door and knock; if anyone hears my voice and opens the door, I will come in to him.' He will have no difficulty in entering; no barrier of closed doors was able to shut out his body after he had risen from the dead. Suddenly, unexpectedly, he was present in the room where the apostles were gathered. He has already tested the apostles; he wants now to test your zeal and devotion. In time of persecution, he may take the initiative; where all is tranquil, he wants you to be ready and waiting for him.

Be on the watch before the sun is visible in the sky. 'Awake, sleeper, and rise from the dead, so that Christ may shine on you.' If you are vigilant, you will receive Christ's light before sunrise. Before daybreak, he will shine into the depth of your heart. Even as you say: 'My spirit watches for you in the night', Christ will make the light of morning illuminate your nocturnal meditation on the word of God. As you meditate, light will dawn. Seeing that light – not of the day but of grace – you will exclaim: 'Your commandments are my light!' When day finds you meditating on God's word and the pleasant task of prayer and psalmody delights your mind, you will once more say to the Lord Jesus: 'You fill both morning and evening with joy.'

St Augustine (354-430)

PICK IT UP, READ IT; PICK IT UP, READ IT!

St Augustine was born in Thagaste in North Africa. Despite the example of his devout Christian mother, he became a Manichean. The Manicheans, who had been founded by the prophet Mani in the third century AD, believed in a struggle between a good, spiritual world of light, and an evil, material world of darkness. The young Augustine's journey to his mother's deep faith in Jesus Christ was a long and painful process. In this passage from his Confessions (VIII, 28), *Augustine tells how, while engaged in a random reading of St Paul's letters, he was suddenly given the grace of full certainty and his doubt vanished. Alypius was a student of Augustine's who became a lifelong friend, 'the brother of his heart'. In 384 he joined Augustine in Milan, where they were both awed by the preaching of St Ambrose. They would be baptized together by Ambrose at the Easter Vigil in April 387.*

On a certain day ... there came to visit Alypius and me at our house one Ponticianus, a fellow countryman of ours from Africa, who held high office in the emperor's court. ... we sat down to talk together, and it chanced that he noticed a book on a game table before us. He took it up, opened it, and, contrary to his expectation, found it to be the apostle Paul, for he imagined that it was one of my wearisome rhetoric textbooks. When I had told him that I had given much attention to these writings, a conversation followed in which he spoke of Antony, the Egyptian monk, whose name was in high repute among thy servants, although up to that time not familiar to me.

But while he was speaking, thou, O Lord, turned me toward myself, taking me from behind my back, where I had put myself while unwilling to exercise self-scrutiny. And now thou didst set me face to face with myself, that I might see how ugly I was, and how crooked and sordid, bespotted and ulcerous. And I looked and I loathed myself; but whither to fly from myself I could not discover. And if I sought to turn my gaze away from myself, he would continue his narrative, and thou wouldst oppose me to myself and thrust me before my own eyes that I might discover my iniquity and hate it. I had known it, but acted as though I knew it not – I winked at it and forgot it.

In the midst, then, of this great strife of my inner dwelling, which I had strongly raised up against my soul in the chamber of my heart, troubled both in mind and countenance, I seized upon Alypius, and exclaimed: 'What is wrong with us? What is this?'

Now when deep reflection had drawn up out of the secret depths of my soul all my misery and had heaped it up before the sight of my heart, there arose a mighty storm, accompanied by a mighty rain of tears. That I might give way fully to my tears and lamentations, I stole away from Alypius, for it seemed to me that solitude was more appropriate for the business of weeping. I went far enough away that I could feel that even his presence was no restraint upon me. This was the way I felt at the time, and he realized it. I suppose I had said something before I started up and he noticed that the sound of my voice was choked with weeping. And so he stayed alone, where we had been sitting together, greatly astonished. I flung myself down under a fig tree – how I know not – and gave free course to my tears. The streams of my eyes gushed out an acceptable sacrifice to thee. And, not indeed in these words, but to this effect, I cried to thee: 'And thou, O Lord, how long? How long, O Lord? Wilt thou be angry forever? Oh, remember not against us our former iniquities.' For I felt that I was still enthralled by them. I sent up these sorrowful cries: 'How long, how long? Tomorrow and tomorrow? Why not now? Why not this very hour make an end to my uncleanness?'

I was saying these things and weeping in the most bitter contrition of my heart, when suddenly I heard the voice of a boy or a girl I know not which – coming from the neighbouring house, chanting over and over again, 'Pick it up, read it; pick it up, read it.' Immediately I ceased weeping and began most earnestly to think whether it was usual for children in some kind of game to sing such a song, but I could not remember ever having heard the like. So, damming the torrent of my tears, I got to my feet, for I could not but think that this was a divine command to open the Bible and read the first passage I should light upon. For I had heard how Antony, accidentally coming into church while the gospel was being read, received the admonition as if what was read had been addressed to him: 'Go and sell what you have and give it to the poor, and you shall have treasure in heaven; and come and follow me.' By such an oracle he was forthwith converted to thee.

So I quickly returned to the bench where Alypius was sitting, for there I had put down the apostle's book when I had left there. I snatched it up, opened it, and in silence read the paragraph on which my eyes first fell: 'Not in partying and drunkenness, not in promiscuity and shamelessness, not in fighting and jealousy, but clothe yourself in the Lord Jesus Christ and make no provision for the flesh concerning its physical desires' (Romans 13: 13-14). I wanted to read no further, nor did I need to. For instantly, as the sentence ended, there was infused in my heart something like the light of full certainty and all the gloom of doubt vanished away.

Closing the book, then, and putting in my finger or something else for a mark, I began – now with a tranquil countenance – to tell it all to Alypius. And he in turn disclosed to me what had been going on in himself, of which I knew nothing. He asked to see what I had read. I showed him, and he looked on even further than I had read. I had not known what followed. But indeed it was this, 'Receive the one who is weak in faith' (Romans 14: 1). This he applied to himself, and told me so. By these words of warning he was strengthened, and by exercising his good resolution and purpose – all very much in keeping with his character, in which, in these respects, he was always far different from and better than I – he joined me in full commitment without any restless hesitation.

St Gregory the Great (*c.*540-604)

LEARN TO KNOW THE HEART OF GOD IN THE WORDS OF GOD.

St Gregory the Great was pope from 590 to 604. He wrote the only account we have of the life of St Benedict and sent St Augustine and his fellow monks to England to convert the Anglo-Saxons. Here he writes to Theodore, who was physician to the Emperor Maurice in Constantinople. He begins his letter by thanking Theodore for the money he has sent to ransom captives, and now reminds him of his urgent need still better to learn to know and love Christ, his Redeemer who ransoms him for eternal life. (Epist. IV, 31 (PL 77, 706ab))

Since one who loves more risks more, I must reprimand my most illustrious son Theodore. He has received from the most holy Trinity the gifts of intelligence, well-being, mercy and charity. But they are forever being stifled by profane questions, by constant comings and goings. Thus he neglects to read the words of his Redeemer each day. What is Scripture if not a letter from almighty God to his creature? If your Excellency lived somewhere else and received a letter from an earthly monarch, he would have no peace, he would not rest, he would not shut his eyes until he had learned the contents of that letter. The King of Heaven, the Lord of Men and Angels, has written you a letter that you might live, and yet, illustrious son, you neglect to read it with ardent love. Strive therefore, I beg you, to meditate each day on the words of your Creator. Learn to know the heart of God in the words of God. Thus you will long for the things of heaven with greater desire, and your soul will be more eager for the joys that are celestial. Then will your rest be so much the greater as now you have been restless for love of your Creator. May the Spirit fill your soul with his presence, and, in filling it, make it lighter.

St Dominic (1170-1221)

HE WOULD BE MOVED IN HIS MIND AS DELIGHTFULLY AS IF HE HEARD THE LORD SPEAKING TO HIM.

St Dominic was born at Caleruega in Spain. He became a Canon Regular of Osma. In 1206 he was sent to Languedoc to combat the Catharist or Albigensian heresy. To help in this work he founded the Order of Preachers (the Dominicans); they were approved by the Holy See in 1216 and have had an immense impact on the life of the Church. Here a contemporary disciple describes St Dominic engaged in Lectio (From The Nine Ways of Prayer of Saint Dominic, *translated by Simon Tugwell, O.P.)*

Sitting there quietly, he would open some book before him, arming himself first with the sign of the cross, and then he would read. And he would be moved in his mind as delightfully as if he heard the Lord speaking to him. As the Psalm says, 'I will hear what the Lord God is saying in me, because he will speak peace to his people and upon his saints, and to those who turn to him with all their heart' (Psalm 85 [84]: 8). It was as if he were arguing with a friend; at one moment he would appear to be feeling impatient, nodding his head energetically, then he would seem to be listening quietly, then you would see him disputing and struggling, and laughing and weeping all at once, fixing then lowering his gaze, then again speaking quietly and beating his breast. If anyone was inquisitive enough to want to spy on him secretly, he would find that the holy father Dominic was like Moses, who went into the innermost desert and saw the burning bush and the Lord speaking and calling to him to humble himself (Exodus 3: 1ff). The man of God had a prophetic way of passing over quickly from reading to prayer and from meditation to contemplation. When he was reading like this on his own, he used to venerate the book and bow to it and sometimes kiss it, particularly if it was a book of the gospels or if he was reading the words which Christ had spoken with his own lips. And sometimes he used to hide his face and turn it aside, or he would bury his face in his hands or hide it a little in his scapular. And then he would also become anxious and full of yearning, and he would also rise a little, respectfully, and bow as if he were thanking some very special person for favours received. Then, quite refreshed and at peace in himself, he would continue reading his book.

St Francis of Assisi (1181/2 – 1226)

GO AND DO AS THOU HAST HEARD.

St Francis was the son of a wealthy merchant in Assisi. Called by God, he embraced a life of poverty and preached to all the love of God. In 1210, Innocent III approved his Order of Friars Minor (the Franciscans). Two years later he helped St Clare establish the Poor Clares. In 1224, while praying at La Verna, he received the wounds of Christ crucified. This passage is from The Little Flowers of St Francis, *probably written by one of the Friars Minor, Ugolino Brunforte (c. 1262- c.1348).*

Then Bernard … was touched by the Holy Spirit, and resolved to change his life. Next morning, therefore, he called St Francis, and thus addressed him: 'Brother Francis, I am disposed in heart wholly to leave the world, and to obey thee in all things as thou shalt command me.' At these words, St Francis rejoiced in spirit and said, 'Bernard, a resolution such as thou speakest of is so difficult and so great an act, that we must take counsel of the Lord Jesus Christ, and pray to him that he may be pleased to show us what is his will, and may teach us to follow it. Let us then go together to the Bishop's palace, where we shall find a good priest who will say Mass for us. We will then remain in prayer till the third hour, imploring the Lord to point out to us the way he wishes us to select, and to this intent we will open the Missal three times.' And when Bernard answered that he was well pleased with this proposal, they set out together, heard Mass, and after they had remained in prayer till the time fixed, the priest, at the request of St Francis, took up the Missal, then, having made the sign of the holy cross, he opened it three times, in the name of our Lord Jesus Christ. The first place which he lit upon was at the answer of Christ to the young man who asked of him the way to perfection: 'If thou wilt be perfect, go, sell all that thou hast and give to the poor, and come, follow me.' The second time he opened at the words which the Saviour addressed to the Apostles when he sent them forth to preach the Word of Truth: 'Take nothing with you for your journey: neither staff, nor scrip, nor bread, nor money';

wishing to teach them thereby to commit the care of their lives to him, and give all their thoughts to the preaching of the Holy Gospel. When the Missal was opened a third time they came upon these words: 'If anyone will come after me, let him deny himself, and take up his cross, and follow me.' Then St Francis, turning to Bernard, said: 'This is the advice that the Lord has given us; go and do as thou hast heard; and blessed be the Lord Jesus Christ who has pointed out to thee the way of his angelic life.' Upon this, Bernard went and sold all that he had. Now he was very rich, and with great joy he distributed his wealth to widows, to orphans, to prisoners, to monasteries, to hospitals, and to pilgrims, in all which St Francis assisted him with prudence and fidelity.

St Bonaventure (1221-1274)

THE SUBSTANCE AND FRUIT OF HOLY SCRIPTURE IS VERY SPECIFIC: THE FULLNESS OF ETERNAL HAPPINESS.

St Bonaventure was the seventh Minister General of St Francis's Order of Friars Minor. He is a Doctor of the Church, being known as the Seraphic Doctor. As a small child, he was saved from death by St Francis's prayers. The following passage is from the Breviloquium (Prologus: Opera Omnia 5, 201-202); *it was probably completed in 1257 and has been called a 'precious jewel box' of mediaeval thought.*

The stream of holy Scripture flows not from human research but from revelation by God. It springs from the *Father of lights, from whom all fatherhood in heaven and on earth takes its name* (James 1:17; Ephesians 3:15). From him, through his Son Jesus Christ, the Holy Spirit flows into us; and through the Holy Spirit, giving, at will, different gifts to different people, comes the gift of faith, and, through faith, Jesus Christ has his dwelling in our hearts. This is the knowledge of Jesus Christ, which is the ultimate basis of the solidity and wisdom of the whole of holy Scripture.

From all this it follows that it is impossible for anyone to start to recognise Scripture for what it is if he does not already have faith in Christ infused into him. Christ is the lamp that illuminates the whole of Scripture: he is its gateway and its foundation. For this faith is behind all the supernatural enlightenments that we receive while we are still separated from the Lord and on our pilgrimage. It makes our foundation firm, it directs the light of the lamp, it leads us in through the gateway. It is the standard against which the wisdom that God has given us should be measured, so that *no-one should exaggerate his real importance, but everyone must judge himself soberly by the standard of the faith God has given him* (Romans 12:3).

The substance and fruit of holy Scripture is very specific: the fullness of eternal happiness. For this is what Scripture is – its words are words of eternal life, and it is written not just so that we should believe, but specially so that we should possess eternal life in which we may see, and love, and have all our desires fulfilled. When they are fulfilled, then we shall know the superabundant love that comes from knowledge, and so we shall be filled with all the fullness of God. God's Scripture tries to lead us to this fullness, and to the truth of the preaching of the apostles. It is to this end, with this intention, that we should study holy Scripture, and teach it, and hear it.

If we are to follow the direct path of Scripture and come straight to the final destination, then right from the beginning – when simple faith starts to draw us towards the light of the Father – our hearts should kneel down and ask the Father to give us, through his Son and the Holy Spirit, true knowledge of Jesus and of his love. Once we know him and love him like this, we shall be made firm in faith and deeply rooted in love, and we can know the breadth, length, depth and height of holy Scripture. That news can then lead us to the full knowledge and overwhelming love of the most holy Trinity. The desires of the saints draw them towards the Trinity, in which all that is good and true is and finds its completion.

St Thérèse of Lisieux (1873-1897)

O JESUS, MY LOVE, AT LAST I HAVE FOUND MY CALLING: MY CALL IS LOVE.

St Thérèse Martin joined her two sisters in the Carmel of Lisieux when she was only fifteen. She died of tuberculosis at the age of twenty-four. In spite of her short life, her spiritual writings and her 'little way' have had so great an influence that St John Paul II declared her a Doctor of the Church in 1997. This passage is taken from The Autobiography of St

Thérèse of the Child Jesus (Manuscrits autobiographiques, 1957, 227-229).

Since my longing for martyrdom was powerful and unsettling, I turned to the epistles of St Paul in the hope of finally finding an answer. By chance, the twelfth and thirteenth chapters of the first epistle to the Corinthians caught my attention, and in the first section I read that not everyone can be an apostle, prophet or teacher, that the Church is composed of a variety of members, and that the eye cannot be the hand. Even with such an answer revealed before me, I was not satisfied and did not find peace.

I persevered in the reading and did not let my mind wander until I found this encouraging theme: 'Set your desires on the greater gifts. And I will show you the way which surpasses all others' (1 Corinthians 12: 31). For the Apostle insists that the greater gifts are nothing at all without love and that this same love is surely the best path leading directly to God. At length I had found peace of mind.

When I had looked upon the mystical body of the Church, I recognized myself in none of the members that St Paul described, and what is more, I desired to distinguish myself more favourably within the whole body. Love appeared to me to be the hinge for my vocation.

Indeed, I knew that the Church had a body composed of various members, but in this body the necessary and more noble member was not lacking; I knew that the Church had a heart and that such a heart appeared to be aflame with love. I knew that one love drove the members of the Church to action, that if this love were extinguished, the apostles would have proclaimed the Gospel no longer, the martyrs would have shed their blood no more. I saw and realized that love sets off the bounds of all vocations, that love is everything, that this same love embraces every time and every place. In one word, that love is everlasting.

Then, nearly ecstatic with the supreme joy in my soul, I proclaimed: O Jesus, my love, at last I have found my calling: my call is love. Certainly I have found my place in the Church, and you gave me that very place, my God. In the heart of the Church, my mother, I will be love, and thus I will be all things, as my desire finds its direction.

St Teresa of Los Andes (1900-1920)

I LONG FOR YOU TO KNOW HIM SO AS TRULY TO LOVE HIM

Juana Fernández Solar was born in Santiago de Chile in 1900. When she was 18, she entered the novitiate of the Discalced Carmelites in Los Andes and was given the name Teresa de Jesús. Towards the end of her life, which she believed would be short, she began an apostolate of letter writing. She contracted typhus, which was diagnosed as fatal. She may, in fact, have caught the Spanish 'flu, which was devastating Chile at that time. She was given the grace of certainty that her mission to make God known and loved would continue in eternity. This letter to a friend is dated 2nd October 1919. She died on 12th April 1920.

My dear friend,

As we get to know this God-Man, we begin to love him madly. I wish you knew him, so that you would truly fall in love.

The Carmelite lives so familiarly united to him that there is no difference for her between the time when he lived on earth and his life in the tabernacle. There she meets him and, like the Magdalene, she listens to his words of life. And what are those words? The words of the Gospel. In silence the Carmelite savours that teaching, so pure and full of love. There she sees, portrayed in magnificent images, the Saviour, the Word made flesh. She sees her God undergoing the suffering of humanity: enduring the cold in the manger, suffering exile in Egypt, obeying his creatures, he who is almighty. She sees that Child crying in the arms of his poor Mother; and those cries are the sobbing of the one who is limitless Joy.

How can we not love this Jesus with all our soul? Him, who is the uncreated Beauty; him, the eternal Wisdom; him, who is Goodness, Life, Love. How can the soul not burn with love at the sight of that God who is dragged through the streets of Jerusalem with the cross upon his shoulders, at the sight of that God who makes himself into food for his creatures, makes himself bread to unite himself with them, to make them divine and change them into himself?

Oh, love Jesus! Who can better reciprocate your love? He thirsts for your heart. Do you not hear him when, after

Holy Communion, he says: 'Daughter, give me your heart'? God, whole and infinite, is begging for a poor, mean heart, for whose sake he poured out all his blood, for whose sake he has made himself bread to feed you. Live with him in the intimacy of your soul. 'Anyone who carries out the will of my Father, such a one loves me and I and my Father will love him and we will come to him and make our home within him' (cf. John 14: 23). This is what Jesus says to you. So carry out your part and you will live with him there, in your soul as though in a cell. And you will be able to hear and see him every moment of the day.

Good-bye.

I, your unworthy friend, entrust you to him.

Etty Hillesum (1914-1943)

THE LORD IS MY HIGH TOWER

Our last witness to the power of God's Word was a young Jewish woman who, like Edith Stein (St Teresa Benedicta of the Cross), made the journey from atheism to deep faith in the terrible circumstances of the Jewish community leading up to and during the Holocaust. The first quotation is from a long letter she wrote in the transit camp at Westerbork, from which 100,000 Jews were sent to their deaths in the extermination camps of the East. Just as for St Thérèse of Lisieux, reading St Paul's first letter to the Corinthians (13: 1ff.) brought about in Etty a transforming discovery in Christ.

I know that those who hate have good reason to do so. But why should we always have to choose the cheapest and easiest way? It has been brought home forcibly to me here how every atom of hatred added to the world makes it an even more inhospitable place. And I also believe, childishly perhaps but stubbornly, that the earth will become more habitable again only through the love that the Jew Paul described to the citizens of Corinth in the thirteenth chapter of his first letter.

This second quotation is from a postcard Etty wrote to a friend, Christine van Nooten, which she threw from the train that was taking her and her family to Auschwitz. Farmers picked it up and sent it on. Etty died in Auschwitz on 30th November 1943. We can finish our time with these witnesses to the power of the Word by reading Psalm 18 (Psalm 17 in the Catholic tradition) with the ear of the heart.

Christine,

Opening the Bible at random, I find this: 'The Lord is my high tower' (Psalm 18 [17]: 2). I am sitting on my rucksack in the middle of a full freight car. Father, Mother and Mischa (her brother) are a few cars away. In the end, the departure came without warning. On sudden special orders from the Hague. We left the camp singing, Father and Mother, firmly and calmly, Mischa too... Good-bye for now from the four of us. Etty.

VII. The Teaching of the Church on Lectio Divina

Church Councils and the Popes in their teaching have encouraged the faithful to grow in their love and knowledge of God's word. Here are some passages to guide and inspire your faithful practice of Lectio Divina. You will be able to find the full texts online at www.vatican.va

None can fail to see what profit and sweet tranquillity must result in well-disposed souls from such devout reading of the Bible. Whosoever comes to it in piety, faith and humility, and with determination to make progress in it, will assuredly find therein and will eat the 'Bread that cometh down from heaven' (John 6: 33); he will, in his own person, experience the truth of David's words: 'The hidden and uncertain things of thy Wisdom thou hast made manifest to me!' (Psalm 50: 8), for this table of the Divine Word does really 'contain holy teaching, teach the true faith, and lead us unfalteringly beyond the veil into the Holy of Holies.' Hence, as far as in us lies, we, Venerable Brethren, shall, with St Jerome as our guide, never desist from urging the faithful to read daily the Gospels, the Acts and the Epistles, so as to gather thence food for their souls.

Our one desire for all the Church's children is that, being saturated with the Bible, they may arrive at the all-surpassing knowledge of Jesus Christ.

Benedict XV, *Spiritus Paraclitus* (nn. 43 & 69), 1920

The Church has always venerated the divine Scriptures just as she venerates the body of the Lord; she unceasingly receives and offers to the faithful the bread of life from the table both of God's word and of Christ's body ... In the sacred books, the Father who is in heaven meets his children with great love and speaks with them; and the force and power in the word of God is so great that it stands as the support and energy of the Church, the strength of faith for her sons, the food of the soul, the pure and everlasting source of spiritual life.

Vatican II, *Dei Verbum (n. 21), 1965*

Only by the light of faith and by meditation on the word of God can one always and everywhere recognize God in whom 'we live, and move, and have our being' (Acts 17:28), seek his will in every event, see Christ in everyone, whether he be a relative or a stranger, and make correct judgments about the true meaning and value of temporal things, both in themselves and in their relation to man's final goal.

Vatican II, *Apostolicam Actuositatem* (n. 4), 1965

The word of God is the first source of all Christian spirituality. It gives rise to a personal relationship with the living God and with his saving and sanctifying will. It is for this reason that from the very beginning of Institutes of Consecrated Life, and in a special way in monasticism, what is called Lectio Divina has been held in the highest regard. By its means, the word of God is brought to bear on life, on which it projects the light of that wisdom which is a gift of the Spirit. Although the whole of Sacred Scripture is 'profitable for teaching' (2 Timothy 3: 16), and is 'the pure and perennial source of spiritual life', the writings of the New Testament deserve special veneration, especially the Gospels, which are 'the heart of all the Scriptures'.

Meditation of the Bible in common is of great value. When practised according to the possibilities and circumstances of life in community, this meditation leads to a joyful sharing of the riches drawn from the word of God, thanks to which brothers or sisters grow together and help one another to make progress in the spiritual life. Indeed it would be helpful if this practice were also encouraged among other members of the People of God, priests and laity alike. This will lead, in ways proper to each person's particular gifts, to setting up schools of prayer, of spirituality and of prayerful reading of the Scriptures, in which God 'speaks to people as friends (cf. Exodus 33:11; John 15: 14-15) and lives among them (cf. Baruch 3: 38), so that he may invite and draw them into fellowship with himself'. The Church's spiritual tradition teaches that meditation on God's word, and on the mysteries of Christ in particular, gives rise to fervour in contemplation and the ardour of apostolic activity. Both in contemplative and active religious life it has always been men and women of prayer, those who truly interpret and put into practice the will of God, who do great works. From familiarity with God's word they draw the light needed for that individual and communal discernment which helps them to seek the ways of the Lord in the signs of the times. In this way they acquire a kind of supernatural intuition, which allows them to avoid being conformed to the mentality of this world, but rather to be renewed in their own mind, in order to discern God's will about what is good, perfect and pleasing to him (cf. Romans 12: 2).

St John Paul II, *Vita Consecrata* (n. 94), 1996

The primary aim of evangelization is Sacred Scripture: in concrete terms, catechesis should be an authentic introduction to Lectio Divina, that is, to a reading of the Sacred Scriptures, done according to the Spirit who dwells in the Church.

Directorium Generale pro Catechesi (n. 127), 1997

'I am the Way, the Truth and the Life' (John 14: 6). With these words, Jesus presents himself as the one path that leads to holiness. But a specific knowledge of this way comes chiefly through the word of God, which the Church proclaims in her preaching. Therefore, the Church in America 'must give a clear priority to prayerful reflection on Sacred Scripture by all the faithful'. This reading of the Bible, accompanied by prayer, is known in the tradition of the Church as Lectio Divina, and it is a practice to be encouraged among all Christians. For priests, Lectio Divina must be a basic feature of the preparation of their homilies, especially the Sunday homily.

> St John Paul II, *Ecclesia in America* (n. 31), 1999

The Church lives on the word of God and the word of God echoes through the Church, in her teaching and throughout her life. In this context, I would like in particular to recall and recommend the ancient tradition of Lectio Divina: the diligent reading of Sacred Scripture, accompanied by prayer, brings about that intimate dialogue in which the person reading hears God who is speaking, and in praying, responds to him with trusting openness of heart (cf. *Dei Verbum*, n. 25). If it is effectively promoted, this practice will bring to the Church – I am convinced of it – a new spiritual springtime.

> Benedict XVI, on the Fortieth Anniversary of *Dei Verbum*, 2005

Sacred Scripture introduces one into communion with the family of God. Thus, one should not read Sacred Scripture on one's own. Of course, it is always important to read the Bible in a very personal way, in a personal conversation with God; but at the same time, it is important to read it in the company of people with whom one can advance, letting oneself be helped by the great masters of Lectio Divina. ... These teachers help us to understand better and also to learn how to interpret Sacred Scripture properly. Moreover, it is also appropriate in general to read it in the company of friends who are journeying with me, who are seeking, together with me, how to live with Christ, to find what life the word of God brings us. If it is important to read Sacred Scripture with the help of teachers and in the company of friends, travelling companions, it is particularly important to read it in the great company of the pilgrim People of God, that is, in the Church.

Benedict XVI, *Meeting with the Youth of Rome in Preparation for the Twenty-first World Youth Day, 2006*

My dear young friends, I urge you to become familiar with the Bible, and to have it at hand, so that it can be your compass, pointing out the road to follow. By reading it, you will learn to know Christ.

Benedict XVI, *Final Message of the World Youth Day, 2006*

How can we truly know Christ so as to be able to follow him and live with him, so as to find life in him and to communicate that life to others, to society and to the world? First and foremost, Christ makes his person, his life and his teaching known to us through the word of God. At the beginning of this new phase that the missionary Church of Latin America and the Caribbean is preparing to enter, starting with this Fifth General Conference in Aparecida, an indispensable pre-condition is profound knowledge of the word of God.

To achieve this, we must train people to read and meditate on the word of God: this must become their staple diet, so that, through their own experience, the faithful will see that the words of Jesus are spirit and life (cf. John 6:63). Otherwise, how could they proclaim a message whose content and spirit they do not know thoroughly? We must build our missionary commitment and the whole of our lives on the rock of the word of God. For this reason, I encourage the Bishops to strive to make it known.

Benedict XVI *Address at the Inaugural Session of Aparecida Conference* (3 Disciples and Missionaries), 2007

We must never forget that the word of God transcends time. Human opinions come and go. What is very modern today will be very antiquated tomorrow. On the other hand, the word of God is the word of eternal life, it bears within it eternity and is valid forever. By carrying the word of God within us, we therefore carry within us eternity, eternal life.

I thus conclude with a word St Jerome once addressed to St Paulinus of Nola. In it, the great exegete expressed this very reality, that is, in the word of God we receive eternity, eternal life. St Jerome said: 'Seek to learn on earth those truths which will remain ever valid in heaven' (Ep. 53, 10).

Benedict XVI, *General Audience on St Jerome*, 2007

The word that opens the path of that search, and is to be identified with this path, is a shared word. True, it pierces every individual to the heart (cf. Acts 2: 37). Gregory the

Great describes this as a sharp stabbing pain, which tears open our sleeping soul and awakens us, making us attentive to the essential reality, to God. But in the process, it also makes us attentive to one another. The word does not lead to a purely individual path of mystical immersion, but to the pilgrim fellowship of faith.

Benedict XVI *Address at the Meeting with the Representatives from the World of Culture, 2008*

It is the word that forms history, reality. Furthermore, the word of God is the foundation of everything, it is the true reality. And to be realistic, we must rely upon this reality. We must change our idea that matter, solid things, things we can touch, are the more solid, the more certain reality. At the end of the Sermon on the Mount, the Lord speaks to us about the two possible foundations for building the house of one's life: sand and rock. The one who builds on sand builds only on visible and tangible things, on success, on career, on money. Apparently these are the true realities. But all this one day will pass away. We can see this now with the fall of large banks: this money disappears, it is nothing. And thus all things, which seem to be the true realities we can count on, are only realities of a secondary order. The one who builds his life on these realities, on matter, on success, on appearances, builds upon sand. Only the word of God is the foundation of all reality, it is as stable as the heavens and more than the heavens, it is reality. Therefore, we must change our concept of realism. The realist is the one who recognizes the word of God, in this apparently weak reality, as the foundation of all things. Realist is the one who builds his life on this foundation, which is permanent.

Benedict XVI *Address at the Opening of the 12th Synod of Bishops,* 2008

Listening together to the word of God, engaging in biblical Lectio Divina, letting ourselves be struck by the inexhaustible freshness of God's word which never grows old, overcoming our deafness to those words that do not fit our own opinions or prejudices, listening and studying within the communion of the believers of every age: all these things represent a way of coming to unity in faith as a response to hearing the word of God.

...it is clear that Scripture itself points us towards an appreciation of its own unbreakable bond with the Eucharist. 'It can never be forgotten that the divine word, read and proclaimed by the Church, has as its one purpose the sacrifice of the new covenant and the banquet of grace, that is, the Eucharist'. Word and Eucharist are so deeply bound together that we cannot understand one without the other: the word of God sacramentally takes flesh in the event of the Eucharist. The Eucharist opens us to an understanding of Scripture, just as Scripture for its part illumines and explains the mystery of the Eucharist. Unless we acknowledge the Lord's real presence in the Eucharist, our understanding of Scripture remains imperfect.

...I would also like to echo what the Synod proposed about the importance of the personal reading of Scripture, also as a practice allowing for the possibility, in accordance with the Church's usual conditions, of gaining an indulgence either for oneself or for the faithful departed. The practice of indulgences implies the doctrine of the infinite merits of Christ – which the Church, as the minister of the redemption, dispenses and applies, but it also implies that of the communion of saints, and it teaches us that 'to whatever degree we are united in Christ, we are united to one another, and the supernatural life of each one can be useful for the others'. From this standpoint, the reading of the word of God sustains us on our journey of penance and conversion, enables us to deepen our sense of belonging to the Church, and helps us to grow in familiarity with God. As Saint Ambrose puts it, 'When we take up the sacred Scriptures in faith and read them with the Church, we walk once more with God in the Garden'.

Benedict XVI, *Verbum Domini* (nn. 46, 55, 87), 2010

There is one particular way of listening to what the Lord wishes to tell us in his word and of letting ourselves be transformed by the Spirit. It is what we call Lectio Divina. It consists of reading God's word in a moment of prayer and allowing it to enlighten and renew us...In the presence of God, during a recollected reading of the text, it is good to ask, for example: 'Lord, what does this text say to me? What is it about my life that you want to change by this text? What troubles me about this text? Why am I not interested in this?' Or perhaps: 'What do I find pleasant in this text? What is it about this word that moves me? What attracts me? Why does it attract me?'

When we make an effort to listen to the Lord, temptations usually arise. One of them is simply to feel troubled or burdened, and to turn away. Another common temptation is to think about what the text means for other people, and so avoid applying it to our own life. It can also happen that we look for excuses to water down the clear meaning of the text. Or we can wonder if God is demanding too much of us, asking for a decision which we are not yet prepared to make. This leads many people to stop taking pleasure in the encounter with God's word; but this would mean forgetting that no one is more patient than God our Father, that no one is more understanding and willing to wait.

He always invites us to take a step forward, but does not demand a full response if we are not yet ready. He simply asks that we sincerely look at our life and present ourselves honestly before him, and that we be willing to continue to grow, asking from him what we ourselves cannot as yet achieve.

Francis, *Evangelii Gaudium* (nn. 152-153), 2014

In order to be capable of mercy, therefore, we must first of all dispose ourselves to listen to the Word of God. This means rediscovering the value of silence in order to meditate on the Word that comes to us. In this way, it will be possible to contemplate God's mercy and adopt it as our lifestyle.

Francis, *Misericordiae Vultus* (n. 13), 2015

One of the most significant elements of monastic life in general is the centrality of the word of God for personal and community life. St Benedict stressed this when he asked his monks to listen willingly to sacred readings: 'lectiones sanctas libenter audire'. Over the centuries, monasticism has been the guardian of Lectio Divina. Nowadays this is commended to the entire People of God and demanded of all consecrated religious. You yourselves are called to make it the nourishment of your contemplation and daily life, so that you can then share this transforming experience of God's word with priests, deacons, other consecrated persons and the laity. Look upon this sharing as a true ecclesial mission.

Prayer and contemplation are certainly the most fitting place to welcome the word of God, yet they themselves have their source in hearing that word. The entire Church, and especially communities completely devoted to contemplation, need to rediscover the centrality of the word of God, which, as my predecessor St John Paul II stated, is the 'first source of all spirituality'. The word of God needs to nourish your life, your prayer, your contemplation and your daily journey, and to become the principle of communion for your communities and fraternities. For they are called to welcome that word, to meditate upon it, to contemplate it and to join in putting it into practice, communicating and sharing the fruits born of this experience. In this way, you will grow in an authentic spirituality of communion. Here I urge you to 'avoid the risk of an individualistic approach, and remember that God's word is given to us precisely to build communion, to unite us in the Truth along our path to God... Consequently, the sacred text must always be approached in the communion of the Church'.

Francis, *Vultum Dei Quaerere* (n. 19), 2016

That word is living and active. At the very beginning of creation, God spoke and the world came to be (cf. Genesis 1: 6-7). In the fullness of time, Jesus gave us words that are 'spirit and life' (John 6: 63). By his word, he restored broken hearts, as in the case of Zacchaeus and the tax collector Matthew, to whom 'he said, "Follow me". And he got up and followed him' (Matthew 9: 9). In these coming days, praying with the Scriptures, you will be able to experience anew the effectiveness of that word: it does not return empty, but accomplishes the purpose for which it was given (cf. Isaiah 55: 10-11). It is my hope that you will always receive the Bible in its precious uniqueness: as a word that, imbued with the Holy Spirit the Giver of life, communicates to us Jesus, who is life (cf. John 14: 6), and thus makes our lives fruitful. No other book has the same power. In its word, we recognize the Spirit who inspired it: for only in the Spirit can Scripture truly be received, lived and proclaimed, for the Spirit teaches all things and reminds us of all that Jesus said (cf. John 14: 26).

God's word is sharp. It is honey, offering the comforting sweetness of the Lord, but also a sword bringing a salutary unrest to our hearts (cf. Revelation 10: 10). For it penetrates to the depths and brings to light the dark recesses of the soul. As it penetrates, it purifies. The double edge of this 'sword' may at first wound, but it proves beneficial, for it cuts away everything that distances us from God and his love. I pray that, through the Bible, you will taste and feel deep within yourselves the Lord's tender love and his healing presence, which searches us and knows us (cf. Psalm 139: 1).

Finally, God's word judges thoughts and intentions. The word of life is also truth (cf. John 14: 6), and his word 'creates' truth in us, dissipating every form of falsehood and duplicity. Scripture constantly challenges us to redirect our path to God. Letting ourselves 'be read' by the word of God thus enables us to become in turn 'open books', living reflections of the saving word, witnesses of Jesus and proclaimers of his newness. For the word of God always brings newness; it is elusive and often breaks through our own plans and preconceptions.

Francis, *Address to the Delegation from the American Bible Society,* 2018

VIII. Seven Helpful Practices

1. Each day find some time, however brief, for your Lectio Divina.
2. Keep a period of silence in which you can awaken to God's presence.
3. Invite the Holy Spirit into your heart.
4. If the Good News comes to you in your Lectio, share your echo. Give your echo in the first person singular. Listen with the ear of the heart to the echoes of others. God is also speaking to you through them.
5. In shared Lectio, refrain from commentary, asking questions or trying to answer those of others. These derail Lectio into a conversation about Jesus as if he were not there.
6. Finish with a moment of thanksgiving and the Our Father.
7. Keep a word or phrase from your Lectio for subsequent rumination and prayer.

IX. Recommended Reading

Bibles

The New Jerusalem Bible (Study Edition) ISBN 0-232-52077-1. This edition of the Bible is invaluable for its footnotes and cross-references, and is the one generally used by members of the Manquehue Apostolic Movement and the Weave of Manquehue Prayer.

The Christian Community Bible (Catholic Pastoral Edition with Study Notes), ISBN 9789719476634 is widely popular.

The Good News Bible (Catholic Edition) ISBN 9780564070879 also has good cross-references and is often used for church, school and personal study.

The Revised Standard Version Catholic Edition ISBN 9780898708332 contains the deuterocanonical books of the Old Testament placed in the traditional order of the Vulgate. Widely used and quoted by Catholic scholars and theologians, it is the version for the scripture quotations in the Catechism of the Catholic Church. The RSV is considered the first ecumenical Bible and brings together the two traditions – the Catholic Douay-Rheims Bible and the Authorized or King James Version.

www.universalis.com This site gives you immediate access to the Biblical readings for every day, and much more.

Lectio Divina

Guigo II, *Scala Claustralium (The Ladder of Monks)*, Cistercian Publications, ISBN 10: 0879077484. This is the classic twelfth-century account of the four stages of Lectio Divina as outlined in this booklet. It is short, simple and profound.

Benedict XVI, *Verbum Domini: Post-Synodal Apostolic Exhortation*, (2010). The guidance in n. 87 is a helpful description of the basic steps of Lectio Divina.

Enzo Bianchi, *Praying the Word: An Introduction to Lectio Divina*, ISBN 10: 0879076828.

Enzo Bianchi, *Lectio Divina: From God's Word to our Lives,* ISBN 9780281073344. Enzo Bianchi writes from a lifetime's experience of Lectio Divina. He has founded an ecumenical monastic community at Bose in Italy that centres on the word of God.

Michael Casey, *Sacred Reading: The Ancient Art of Lectio Divina*, ISBN 9780892438914. This is 'a postgraduate treatment of lectio', written by a Cistercian monk, that is nonetheless practical and accessible. It is especially helpful for those who want to undertake Lectio Continua.

García M. Colombás, *La Lectura de Dios: Aproximación a la Lectio Divina*, Ediciones Monte Casino, Zamora, 1980, ISBN 10: 8485139496. For Spanish readers; the English translation (ISBN 10: 156788010X) is not readily available.

José Manuel Eguiguren, *Waking up to God*, Downside Abbey Press, 2017, ISBN 978-1-898663-19-5. The second chapter (pp. 43-94) is a helpful treatment of the different ways of approaching Lectio Divina, based on the author's wide experience of Lectio with both monks and nuns and laymen, women and children. José Manuel is the founder of the Manquehue Apostolic Movement.

David Foster, *Reading with God: Lectio Divina*, ISBN 0-8264-6084-4. Dom David, a monk of Downside Abbey, accompanies his reader from hearing the Word to living by the Word. His book is written around scripture passages and reflection on them so that the reader begins to practise Lectio Divina even while reading about it.

Archbishop Andrea Mariano Magrassi, *Praying the Bible: An Introduction to Lectio Divina*, ISBN 9780814624463. In his much-admired book, Archbishop Magrassi invites us to venture into the Bible not as tourists but to become inhabitants of the land.

Silent Prayer

The Way of a Pilgrim, translated by Anna Zaranko, edited with an introduction by Andrew Louth, ISBN 978-0-241-20135-0. This anonymous nineteenth-century book is the tale of a pilgrim who wanders Russia in the quest of unceasing prayer. The Jesus Prayer that he discovers is an intense form of *ruminatio* based on the prayer of the tax collector (Luke 18: 13). This is a wonderful book that you are likely to return to many times.

Recommended Reading

Martin Laird, *Into the Silent Land: the Practice of Contemplation*, ISBN 10: 0232526400. This book will help you grow into the silence that opens you ever more fully to God's presence within you and to the word he has to say to you.

The Fathers

Marcellino D'Ambrosio, *When the Church was Young: Voices of the Early Fathers*, ISBN 978-1-61636-777-0. If you have appreciated the quotations from the Fathers you have met in this book D'Ambrosio provides an informative and enjoyable introduction to their world and writings that will deepen your desire to know more of them.

Modern Testimonies to the Power of the Word

'I Have Seen the Lord': Witnesses of an Encounter with the Risen Christ, ISBN 13: 9798554187445 published by The Weave of Manquehue Prayer, Amazon, 2020. This book is a collection of thirty-eight brief testimonies to encounters with Christ; almost all of them relate to the experience of Lectio Divina in communities belonging to or associated with the Manquehue Apostolic Movement.

About the Cover Picture

Sandro Botticelli (*c.* 1445-1510) was in his mid-thirties when he painted *The Madonna of the Book*. Mary sits as the *Sedes Sapientiae* with Jesus, the Word made flesh, on her lap. Botticelli has achieved the beautiful blue of Mary's mantle by using lapis lazuli, which was imported to Florence from Afghanistan. She is attentively reading from the Office of the Blessed Virgin Mary. Her book is open at Prime for Advent, and we can read some of the words of the *Capitulum* from Isaiah 7: 14-15: 'Ecce virgo concipiet ...' – 'Behold, a virgin shall conceive ...' Of course, no such book could have been found in Mary's home in Nazareth, but any family who could afford a book in Botticelli's day would have a copy of the Office of the Blessed Virgin Mary. Children learnt to read with their mothers from such prayer books, and we still talk of 'Primers'. The picture helps us realise that Mary and Jesus used to read the Scriptures in their place and time just as we do in ours.

Jesus is not looking at the book, but, with loving and compassionate concern for his mother, he reads her face. As Mother of God, she has been spared the pangs of childbirth, but she will experience with him the full human anguish and humiliation of the crucifixion. On the shelves rest two closed books, while two others support the bowl of fruit. Books played an increasing role in pictures of Our

Lady from about 1300 onwards. We cannot know the content of the closed books, but their precious bindings and gilded pages indicate how highly they are valued. Together with the books, we see a wooden box; comparison with contemporary paintings suggests that it contains Mary's sewing equipment. Jesus is the embodiment of Wisdom who has come into the world through Mary; her sewing box indicates the constant care she will bestow on him (cf. 1 Samuel 2: 19!). The closed books may point to the mystery of the 'Verbum infans', the paradox of the Word who has yet to speak. It is Jesus' life, death and resurrection that will open the books for us, and in them we will discover God's mysterious plan for our salvation (cf. Revelation 5: 1-5). There is an air of expectation in this picture that makes it a true icon for Advent.

There are other clues. Prime was said at the first hour of the day; dawn light comes through the window with its view that reminds us there is, alongside the Scriptures, a book of Creation from which we can learn. Yet the strongest light seems to emanate from Jesus, who is the Light of the World. In the bowl are cherries that symbolise the blood of Christ, plums that recall the love of mother and child, and figs that tell of the closeness of the Kingdom of God (Luke 21: 29-33). The golden crown of thorns and the three nails the Child holds are probably a later addition. The Mother and Child hold their hands in the same way so that each right hand bestows a blessing on us.

(Photo: Museo Poldi Pezzoli, Milan)

Printed in Great Britain
by Amazon